FIERCE

A small guide to doing BIG things!

GLORIA MARIE

PELCHER

Copyright © 2013 Gloria Marie Pelcher

All rights reserved. No portion of this book may be used or reproduced in any manner whatsoever without written permission of the author or Creative Bluebird except in the case of brief quotations embodied in critical articles and reviews.

Some scripture taken from THE MESSAGE. Copyright © 1993, 1994, 1995, 1996, 2000, 2001, 2002. Used by permission of NavPress Publishing Group.

FIERCE
A small guide to doing BIG things

ISBN-13: 978-0615860008
ISBN-10: 0615860001

Creative Bluebird
www.creativebluebird.com

Cover Design: GLORIA MARIE PELCHER

For book inquiries please visit
creativebluebird.com/contact

FOR THE #DREAMTEAM

We will live our dreams!

"Walk with the dreamers, the believers, the courageous, the cheerful, the planners, the doers, the successful people with their heads in the clouds and their feet on the ground. Let their spirit ignite a fire within you to leave this world better than when you found it..."

Wilfred Peterson

CONTENTS

INTRODUCTION	1
FAITH	13
INTENT	25
EDUCATION	37
RESILIENCE	45
COMMITMENT	53
EVALUATION	63
CONCLUSION	71
JOURNAL	72
WORKSHOP NOTES	111

INTRODUCTION

Around my 30th birthday God did some incredible things in my life, and people wanted to know the inside workings of the things that were happening. I am a writer at heart, and so only naturally would I write it all out! From conversations I published the eBook *A Guide to Doing Incredible Things With Your Life*. I hoped the eBook would inspire people to position themselves in a place where God could do incredible things in their lives as well.

The feedback I received from readers of the eBook was positive. However, I felt like the book would be more beneficial as a paperback and an interactive journal. When I read over the eBook I saw areas where I could expound more on concepts (and I have definitely done that!), but one of the biggest differences between the eBook and this version is the interactive journal and the title.

One morning I woke up and the subtitle "a small guide to doing big things" literally came out my mouth! It was sort of freaky, but I am one of those people who believe God can speak a word to me by rearranging the letters in my alphabet cereal! The title *FIERCE* comes from an acronym used in the eBook, and also used in this book (explanation on page 4).

For many years I have played it small, but I am so done with playing it small. DONE. We are all created in the image of God, and through him we have the power to accomplish goals, achieve dreams, and live our purpose. It is time to rise up, do big things, and to be FIERCE.

I love encouraging people to dream, to go out there and live their craziest dreams, but dreams mean nothing if you don't work them and believe in them. Before proceeding further I want you to think about two questions. Two very important questions!

The first question deals with working your dreams and the second question deals with believing in your dreams.

❶ Do you wish or work for your dreams?

Many people suffer from a "wishful mentality". They simply wish for things and hope that they will magically come true. Think about a genie, you make your wishes and then the genie makes them come true...in a Disney movie! You live in reality so you can't wish for your dreams you have to work for your dreams. When you suffer from a wishful mentality you strip yourself of your own power, and you don't focus on things inside of your control. Start focusing your energy on things inside of your control. You can control your attitude, you can control your expectations, and you can control your work ethic.

If you have a "wishful mentality" replace it with an "I can do" mentality. The bible says, "I can do all things through Christ who gives me strength." You don't have to wait for some outside force to make the pieces of the puzzle of life fit together; YOU CAN start placing those pieces together yourself. See yourself as equipped to start working towards making your dreams a reality.

❷ Do you believe in your dreams?

I ask this question in relation to your life's purpose. Dreams are related to your life's purpose. Sometimes people chase dreams that are not meant for them and the passion and belief isn't there the way it would be if they were chasing a dream related to their life's purpose. So when I ask, "Do you believe in your dreams?" what I am essentially asking is, "Is the dream you are chasing part of your life's purpose?" Do you believe it is part of God's will for your life?

If you have no idea, take time to discover what it is that you were put on this earth to do! To get started ask God for revelation. If you ask God He will reveal to you His purpose for your life. Think about your passions, what makes you happy, things you would do without pay, things you would do if no one applauds, and be honest with yourself!

T.D. Jakes said it best when he said, "If you can't figure out your purpose, figure out your passion. For your passion will lead you right into your purpose."

Finding your purpose isn't about making others happy. The process of discovering your purpose is about your life, and the purpose that God has for your life.

Make sure you believe 100% in the dreams you are chasing for your life. Make sure your dreams are God-given dreams. You can't be fierce and have doubts about what you do at the same time.

➥ If you answered yes to these two questions, you have more than a dream. You have vision. I challenge you right now to run with it!

THE DIFFERENCE BETWEEN A GOAL AND A DREAM

Dreams are related to your purpose, while goals are related to achieving your dreams. What do I mean? Goals are things that build up to the realization of your dreams. Later on I will go a little more in depth on setting and achieving goals.

HOW THE GUIDE IS SET UP

This guide is set up in 5 sections, based on the acronym F.I.E.R.C.E. In the F.I.E.R.C.E. acronym F stands for faith, I stands for intent, E stands for education, R stands for resilience, C stands for commitment, and E stands for evaluation. These five things will create a shift within your life.

FIERCE isn't a 1-2-3 step program. You can actually start reading at any section. This guide is meant to help you develop a successful mindset, a fierce mindset! Your mindset will influence how you see yourself, it will influence the words that you speak, and ultimately what you will do. The bible says in Proverbs 23:7, "For as he thinketh in his heart, so is he." You are powerful, you are blessed, you are capable, you are equipped, and you are highly favored. You are a mover and shaker.

I want to encourage you, enlighten you, and help you build clarity around the process of living your dreams. My dream is to help you live your dreams, nudge you into a position where you are creating and seizing big opportunities, and declaring greatness and abundance in all areas of your life.

HOW THE INTERACTIVE JOURNAL IS SET UP

The interactive journal is set up with writing prompts. The more you put in the interactive journal the more you will get out of the interactive journal. It is designed to get you actively working towards achieving your dreams and goals. As a writer I know the power of the written word. Written words allow you to think things through, hold you accountable, and releases possibilities.

At the end of the guide there is additional space to write your heart out! Go grab all your colorful highlighters, and your favorite pen! This guide and interactive journal is waiting for you to MAKE YOUR MARK!

What is your biggest dream? Don't downsize your dream. Supersize your faith!

Where do you see yourself in 5 years? Picture how you spend your days.

List at least 5 things you are thankful for in your life:

❶
_____
_____

❷
_____
_____

❸
_____
_____

❹
_____
_____

❺
_____
_____

List at least 5 things you have the power to change in your life:

❶
_____
_____

❷
_____
_____

❸
_____
_____

❹
_____
_____

❺
_____
_____

Describe yourself using only positive adjectives:

(If you're stuck start with the letters in your name for adjectives beginning with those letters!)

What does being fierce and doing big things mean to you?

FIERCE

Write in big letters an inspiring word that will be your go to word for this season of your life!

FAITH

Increase your faith

"Have faith in God; God has faith in you."
Edwin Louis Cole

Faith is paramount in the world of being fierce! It is the foundation which all great things spring from. Things won't always appear all figured out, all sorted and labeled, and perfectly clear in life. It's not that easy. Faith is needed to see things as though they were already made whole, made perfect, made true. Faith is needed to live a blessed life, a life of enrichment and full of God's promises.

It is imperative that you start believing in crazy things. Like exactly what kind of crazy things? How about walking on water? The following is from the book of Matthew from *The Message* bible.

GO AHEAD, BE FEARLESS!

As soon as the meal was finished, he insisted that the disciples get in the boat and go on ahead to the other side while he dismissed the people. With the crowd dispersed, he climbed the mountain so he could be by himself and pray. He stayed there alone, late into the night. Meanwhile, the boat was far out to sea when the wind came up against them and they were battered by the waves. At about four o'clock in the morning, Jesus came toward them walking on the water. They were scared out of their wits. "A ghost!" they said, crying out in terror. But Jesus was quick to comfort them. "Courage, it's me. Don't be afraid." Peter, suddenly bold, said, "Master, if it's really you, call me to come to you on the water." He said, "Come ahead." Jumping out of the boat, Peter walked on the water to Jesus. But when he looked down at the waves churning beneath his feet, he lost his nerve and started to sink. He cried, "Master, save me!" Jesus didn't hesitate. He reached down and grabbed his hand. Then he said, "Faint-heart, what got into you?" The two of them climbed into the boat, and the wind died down. The disciples in the boat, having watched the whole thing, worshiped Jesus, saying, "This is it! You are God's Son for sure!" (Matthew 14:22-33, *The Message*)

Peter asked Jesus to call him to the water, and he was called and Peter walked on water. What do you want God to do in your life? Ask him, and He is willing to give you the desires of your heart. He is willing to call you.

PRAY BOLD PRAYERS

Joel Osteen once had a Facebook status update that said, "If you pray bold prayers God will do bold things in your life." I've been to his church in Houston and I have witnessed firsthand the results of Joel Osteen's bold prayers.

The Message translation of the account of Peter walking on water says that he became bold. Hebrews 4:16 says, "Let us therefore come boldly to the throne of grace, that we may obtain mercy and find grace to help in time of need."

Many people are afraid of being bold because they are afraid of being left out in the middle of the water. It's only natural to ask questions like, "What if I sink?" and "What if I fail?" Without hesitation Jesus will reach out to you, just as He did with Peter when he started to sink.

It is also important to point out the fact that it wasn't until Peter looked down, took his eyes off Jesus (lost his faith), that he started to sink. Keep your focus on the one who walks on water, and get out of your natural into God's supernatural.

Furthermore, some people are afraid to pray bold prayers and go after big things because they are afraid of the change it will bring about in their lives. Change is challenging.

If you are accustomed to one thing all your life, experiencing something greater can be scary. Know that you were born to have dominion and power, you can handle big things. Then you have your haters, not everyone is going to rejoice in the results of your bold prayers. What do you do about the haters? In the south we say, "Bless your heart." Yes, just bless them and move on!

WALK ON WATER?

You might be asking yourself, "Walk on water? Really?" Peter asked Jesus to walk on water, what you want to happen in your life is totally up to you! Matthew 9:29 says, "Then he touch their eyes, saying, According to your faith be it unto you." Your life will unfold according to your faith.

I don't know what your dreams and hopes are in your life, what you dream about at night, but I do know that God is able. Put your faith in God and see the manifestation of His promises.

SHAKE UP YOUR FAITH

Shake up your faith if you are timid about praying and believing God for bold things. Pray the prayer of Jabez (1 Chronicles 4:10) of an enlarged territory starting with your faith.

In different translations of the account of Jesus walking on water Jesus is quoted as saying "oh ye of little faith." Jesus had just fed five thousand people with five loaves of bread and two fish. Like, *you're going to doubt me now?* If you think about it, God has already performed many miracles for you. Build on what God has already done in your life.

Experience the snowball effect with your faith. Once you increase your faith and God starts doing big things in your life you will start to live your life in an elevated dimension. Your faith will continue to increase!

Read Hebrews 11, which is known as the faith chapter, to shift your faith paradigm. Hebrews 11 lists the lives of people who had amazing faith to accomplish miraculous feats.

In Hebrews 11 Sarah is profiled. Sarah was 90 when she had Isaac. Think about that for a moment. 90! I know people in their 30s freaking out because they are yet to bear a child. But get this, Sarah and Abraham waited so long for Isaac and in Genesis 22:2 God tells Abraham to go sacrifice Isaac, and he had so much faith in God that he placed his son on the alter. Think about that for a moment too!

Shaking up your faith has many benefits, including causing others to worship Christ. The scripture says the disciples worshiped Him because they were so amazed at what He had done and what He gave Peter the ability to do. Your faith has the ability to draw others to the wonders of Christ!

➥ What will be your great act of faith? Get in agreement with the plan that God has for your life!

GOD-SIZED DREAMS

In 2011 I told myself that I would move away from imaginable dreams (dreams that I know I can figure out how to accomplish) to unimaginable dreams (dreams I have no idea on exactly how they are going to come true). In other words, God-sized dreams! Dreams only God can make come true!

Don't let go of dreams because you think they are too big, too crazy, and too impossible. With God all things are possible, right? Therefore, why can't He make your desires a reality? Take your place in the Kingdom of God and exercise your faith.

Many people will tell you that you can't do

something, sometimes even yourself, but take no heed to naysayers and the self-doubt that likes to creep into your head.

There are a lot of things that seem impossible out in the world, mainly because they haven't been done before. Everything at some point was accomplished for the first time.

ACT ON IT, GET OUT THE BOAT!

I once heard that faith starts in your feet. If you really believe something can happen you will act upon your belief. You can't just sit back and say I have faith, yet never act on it. Faith is brought to life by your works. Acting upon your faith can be a scary thing, but God wants you to step out of the boat!

Let your actions show expectancy of what you believe God will do in your life. Dr. Martin Luther King, Jr. said, "Take the first step in faith. You don't have to see the whole staircase, just take the first step."

God wants you to have big faith. He wants you to believe in big things. I don't want to stand before God at the end of my life and for Him to ask me, "Faint-heart, what got into you? Why didn't you trust me to do something extraordinary in your life? I had so much planned for you but you never took that act of faith."

Finish This Prayer: God, increase my faith! I believe...

Write about a time you had faith and God came through for you:

Search "faith quotes" online and write down the first few quotes that pop up!

Read Hebrews 11 and write your thoughts about the chapter:

Write out to God your greatest fear about living a life filled with faith. Be honest!

What will your response be to people who say "it can't be done"?

_____
_____
_____
_____
_____
_____
_____
_____
_____
_____
_____
_____
_____
_____
_____
_____

INTENT

Live your life on purpose

"Standing in the inspiring vision of my future, I boldly take every step – large and small – with courage and intent."
Jonathan Lockwood Huie

We hear a lot about living life with intent, it's one of those buzz words that is popping up everywhere, but what does it mean? To live a life of intent everything you do must be done in reflection of some goal or mission.

WRITE A MISSION STATEMENT

Over 10 years ago I wrote out a personal mission statement, things that I do and believe are in alignment with my mission statement. If you have no mission or direction in life someone else is more than willing to take you for a ride. I encourage you to sit down and write a mission statement for your life, this mission statement will define who you are as a person, it will shape how you move about in the world.

In *7 Habits of Effective People for Teens* one of the exercises is to write out a mission statement. The book states how it doesn't have to be elaborate. Your mission statement could be as simple as a bible verse. The bible says to walk humbly before God, and if that is the only thing in your mission statement you will forever be on the right track. Small statements can be profound.

➡ MISSION STATEMENT WRITING TIPS

① Keep It Simple Silly
② Make it personal – no need to please everyone with your mission statement
③ Use adjectives, lots of them!

I have my personal mission statement framed on my desk, a place where I spend a lot of time and a place where I can be reminded daily about my mission. Before framing it I signed it, pretty much to hold myself accountable to the mission. A signature signifies that something is official. It tells the world you stand behind whatever it is that you signed!

BECOME INTENTIONAL

Living a life of intent requires you to be mindful of how you spend your life. In particular, be intentional with your money, your time, and your talents. When you are out to do big things those are the things that can make or break you.

There are people in board rooms trying to figure

out how to entice you to eat what they want you to eat, travel where they want you to travel, watch what they want you to watch, or use the "next great product" that they are selling, and a list of other things. These people make good money attempting to control your most valuable resources

Be Mindful of Your Money: One of the greatest obstacles people think they have between reality and their dreams is the lack of money. I love reading stories of people who start with basically nothing and create a successful business. Starbucks Coffee was started in 1971 with $4,050. Hats off to people who bootstrap it! They make my following statement true: you do not need tons of money to start living your dreams.

Be a good steward of your money. Do you really need another clothing article? Perhaps you could invest that money into classes and materials to build your empire. And yes, you are empire building. All fierce people build empires!

See yourself more as a producer than a consumer. Producers make money. Consumers spend money.

Be Mindful of Your Time: Have you ever wondered how some people get so many things done? They are intentional with their time. They are on a mission 24/7. Productivity is in their vocabulary.

What is your productivity level within your day, your week, your month, and your year? What comes of your time? Think about it.

People say, "I don't have time to do anything. I'm so busy." If you say you are busy and yet you don't have time to do anything, then whatever it is that you are doing amounts to nothing.

Make sure you are not busy with nonproductive things. Is what you are doing with your time moving you closer to your dreams? Consider making a daily schedule, one that fits you and is realistic.

The most common time challenge for people who are out to live their dreams is that they have a full-time job. 40 hours of their week is dedicated to building another man's dream. Yes, if you are not working for yourself you are building someone else's dream!

I recently heard Alastair Humphreys, who is an adventurer (who is also absolutely inspiring), talk about the 5-9. That is all the other time you have away from your full-time job. What are you doing with your 5pm-9am?

If you have a full-time job you have to see yourself as having 2 full-time jobs. I know it's a hard thing to do from personal experience, but I know I must make sacrifices in order to live out my dreams. At the end of your full time job you just want to go home and rest but you have to decide that you want your dreams more than you want to rest, more than you want to watch TV, more than you want to get on social media, more than you want to go hang out, or whatever it is that you do in the evenings after your full-time job.

There is a popular YouTube video by motivational speaker Eric Thomas that asks the question, "How bad do you want it?" He says you have to want it more than you want to breathe. Look up this video and be inspired to give up things to spend time working on your dreams.

I challenge you to cut back on time suckers, anything that sucks a great deal of your time that has nothing to do with reaching your dreams.

If you watch tons of TV cut some of it out of your life and see how much free time you have. I rarely watch television, I watch about 2 hours of TV per week. I like television as much as the next person, but at the end of the day my dream is more important than a TV show. TV is just an example; there are many time wasters out there!

Everyone has moments of minimal motivation, when you just feel like doing nothing at all, and doing nothing at all is okay for a moment but not for a lifestyle.

There is a quote that says the currency of life is time, spend it wisely.

Be Mindful of Your Talent: You are talented! Use your talents. Don't hide them. Being intentional with your talents means responding to and seeking out opportunities where you can use your talents.

Once I had the great experience of writing columns for *The Dallas Morning News* for a year, but in order to get that experience I had to respond to an opportunity.

Whenever good things happen in my life I can always trace back to where I wasn't afraid to put myself out there. Seek out opportunities that will allow you to use your talents.

If there are no opportunities then make them! While the purpose of my blog is to inspire people to dream and live their purpose it is also an opportunity that I created for myself so I can have a place to share my writings.

It's challenging to put yourself out there because everyone is a critic, but putting yourself out there is what allows you to get into your element. Good things come from being in your element. Be brave. Get out there, and make sure the world know who you are and what you do.

GOAL SETTING

Earlier I mentioned the difference between a dream and a goal. Goals are those daily things that you accomplish that add up to your dreams. Being goal oriented is part of living a life of intent.

A popular method of goal setting is the SMART goals model. SMART goals are: specific, measurable, attainable, relevant, and time-bound.

Say one of your goals is to lose weight. Let's go through how a SMART goal sounds: *I want to lose 20 pounds* (specific and attainable) *within the next two months* (time-bound and again attainable), *it's important that I am healthy so I can have energy to do things I want to do* (relevant). *I will eat less and move more, and before long the scale* (measurable) *will reflect my new goal weight!*

A not so smart goal sounds like this: *I want to lose weight.* If your goals sound like that then it's very unlikely that you will accomplish that goal.

MAKE LIFE HAPPEN

Get a plan for your life that aligns with God's plan for your life. Write it out! A modern day proverb says those who fail to plan, plan to fail. You can't let life happen to you, you must make life happen.

It's really easy to get off track and find yourself not far from where you started, but stay the course! Focus, focus, focus on your dreams and life purpose.

God is the founder and owner of my life and he

has appointed me CEO of my life, and I am responsible for making choices every day that accumulate into my successes or my failures.

When you are destined for greatness you must stay away from irrelevant things and let go of anything that keeps you from your destination. Go with God, and not the wind. Think NO DISTRACTIONS, JUST DESTINY.

Finish This Prayer: God, show me how to be more intentional with my life…

Use the space below to write down some ideas for your mission statement:

_____
_____
_____
_____
_____
_____
_____
_____
_____
_____
_____
_____
_____
_____
_____

What can you do in the next week to move closer to your dreams?

_____

_____

_____

_____

_____

_____

_____

_____

_____

_____

_____

_____

_____

_____

A small guide to doing BIG things

List 5 of your biggest time wasters:

❶
_____
_____

❷
_____
_____

❸
_____
_____

❹
_____
_____

❺
_____
_____

List 5 things you want to make part of your daily schedule/routine:

❶
_____
_____

❷
_____
_____

❸
_____
_____

❹
_____
_____

❺
_____
_____

EDUCATION

Become powerful by educating yourself

"Learning is like rowing upstream: not to advance is to drop back."
Chinese Proverb

Going to school and earning a degree is not good enough. It's good, but not good enough if you want to be at the top of your game. If you are into weaving baskets you must become knowledgeable about basket weaving. If you are into playing chess you must become knowledgeable about chess. You must be hungry to learn everything there is to know about whatever it is that you do!

LEARN FROM ONLINE

Having no time or money to learn is not a good excuse to be clueless, FREE information is literally at your fingertips.

I love Google, and if the writing thing doesn't work out I plan to beg Google for a job! If I don't know something I search for it! Not to brag, but I have mad skills when it comes to Google (avoid inferior tools).

How to search online: When looking for information on a search engine pose your search as a question. For example, if I wanted to know why panda bears are so big even though their diet consists mainly of bamboo I would search "why are panda bears so big even though their diet consists of bamboo?" Ask and you will receive (but limit it to 32 words!). And if you are not getting the information you are looking for quickly adjust your search, don't stay with search results if you don't find what you are looking for within the first two pages of results, and move on from pages without valuable information above the first scroll (or in newspaper terms, above the fold).

Consume tons of information at once: You know that broadcast button (that is normally orange) you see on pages? Well, that is the universal logo for a RSS (real simple syndication) feed. If a page has RSS feed you can subscribe to that site/blog using a news reader/aggregator.

Instead of visiting all your favorite blogs and news sites you can go to one central location to read up on all of your topics of interest. It's all the content you are interested in located in one location! The popular news reader/aggregator right now is feedly.com.

On the go when I am not at my computer I use an app called Flipboard on my iPhone and iPad that beautifully presents all my content from across networks. You can add your Facebook, Twitter, etc. accounts to Flipboard. When I am standing in line at the grocery store or when I have other downtime in my life I can catch up on my favorite feeds. I subscribe to content that widens my knowledge in the fields that I work.

Managing all the content you read (or going to start reading!) is a must. There are many RSS readers/aggregators available. Find one that works for you. Having all your content in one place is a good way to consume a ton of online information in a small amount of time.

LEARN FROM PUBLICATIONS IN YOUR FIELD

Besides from being a writer I am also a photographer. I subscribe to 3 different photography magazines, and subscribe to a video photography magazine (Photo Vision). Whatever your field of interest is most likely there is some kind of professional development available through different mediums. Find organizations and publications geared towards your field of interest and find materials that will broaden your understanding and improve your skills.

LEARN FROM OTHERS

A former pastor of mines always says that if you are the smartest one in your group of friends you need some new friends. Agreed! Iron sharpens iron. Make friends with smart interesting people, people who are passionate about their life and work. Their enthusiasm will spill out over on you! These people don't all look like you. Smart comes in all shades, ages, sizes, and backgrounds.

Find people who absolutely love what they do so

much that they want to share everything they know with whoever will listen. Stay away from people who are stingy with their knowledge, people who are afraid to share anything with you because they fear your advancement. You can so do without these types of people.

Follow successful people in and out of your field, study their work. They know a thing or two about success! Learn whatever it is they know that is making them wildly successful. Jasmine Star, Tory Johnson, Michael Hyatt, and Seth Godin are just few of the people I follow.

Be willing to learn from others. Networking and mentorship are vital in personal growth. Part of success is in who you know!

LEARN BY DOING

When I was a kindergarten teacher at the beginning of every year most of my students came to me with terrible handwriting. I gave them tons of opportunities to write and within a matter of months most of their handwriting was pretty darn good. We all start off as beginners when we start doing something and are not very good at the task, but if you keep doing it consistently you are bound to get better.

Carnegie Hall is a prestigious concert venue in Midtown Manhattan, it is a sought after venue for musicians all over the world. There is a popular story about a man being approached by a lost individual on the streets in Midtown Manhattan and being asked, "How do you get to Carnegie Hall?" and the man replies, "Practice, practice, practice."

It's perfectly fine if you suck at first. You will get better. I know practicing can be boring, but if you put in the time you will reap the reward.

LEARN BY TEACHING

When you teach you learn. Some say you don't know something until you teach it. As mentioned, don't hang around people who are stingy with their knowledge, but on the flipside never be stingy with your knowledge. Sharing knowledge never made anyone dumb. Some people are afraid to share information with people because they fear the other person will outdo them. First, this is operating out of fear which is never good. Secondly, they can never be you, and what God has for them is for them and what God has for you is for you. Avoid competition with individuals.

TOO SMART TO BE CLUELESS

You are too smart to be clueless, so get out there and give yourself as many opportunities to learn as you possibly can! Enrich your mind. Invest in self-development to reach your full potential.

My favorite quote is by Abraham Lincoln, "I will prepare, and someday my chance will come." As a teen I printed this quote out and hung it on my wall, and it's about being willing and ready. Be willing to learn and ready for opportunities that come your way.

NEVER stop learning.

Finish This Prayer: God, give me the ability to understand...

List 5 things you want to learn about that will move you closer to your dreams:

❶ _____
_____

❷ _____
_____

❸ _____
_____

❹ _____
_____

❺ _____
_____

List 5 things you know about that you can share with someone or teach to someone:

❶ _____
_____

❷ _____
_____

❸ _____
_____

❹ _____
_____

❺ _____
_____

RESILIENCE

Identify setbacks and recover!

"You may not realize it when it happens, but a kick in the teeth may be the best thing in the world for you."
Walt Disney

From time to time I feel overwhelmed by life, too many things to do and not enough resources, but I have a decree that I will always have a bounce back in my soul. Paula White says that "The devil isn't trying to give you a bad hair day; he is trying to destroy your life!"

Every day you will face opposition, and the opposition is fierce! You will face opposition even more so when you set out to do big things. How are you going to handle it? Vince Lombardi said, "It's not whether you get knocked down, it's whether you get up."

Recovery is a process, and it's okay to cry but not okay to dwell on negative things. Dust yourself off and get back up again. You have too many things to do to waddle in self-pity!

DEVELOP RESILIENCY

Resilience is something you can develop. You can build it up by surrounding yourself with a support system and a thought pattern that lends itself to bouncing back and getting back on track. To obtain resiliency surround yourself with positive energy, positive paraphernalia, and positive people.

POSITIVE ENERGY

Have you ever met someone or heard something that was a total mood crusher?
I believe you can create negative and positive energy, and that it's up to you which one you create. The bible says there is life and death in the tongue. It starts in the tongue.
Create positive energy by speaking positive affirmations to others and to yourself. All the time I tell myself things like "I am more than a conqueror" and "no weapon formed against me shall prosper." Speak and declare the life you want. With your tongue you have the power to change the current atmosphere and the future.

POSITIVE PARAPHERNALIA

I call things in your daily life that reminds you how awesome you are and how anything is possible positive paraphernalia.
Post a favorite quote somewhere in your home that reminds you to overcome situations. When I was in college I posted positive notes on my bathroom mirror. Reading those notes every morning gave me

strength to go rock my day. Today on my bathroom mirror I simply have a sign that reads I CAN.

Jewelry inscribed with positive words and scripture is another way to surround yourself with positive paraphernalia.

POSITIVE PEOPLE

This is somewhat connected to the concept of learning from others. Build up your resilience by surrounding yourself with resilient people. You will feed off their energy.

I once wrote a blog article on where to pitch your tent, because who you sing "Kumbaya" with is important. Avoid holding camp with downers and jealous toxic unmotivated people.

Not everyone is qualified to be part of your life and your destiny. You need people who will speak a positive word into your life, people who will support you when you want to give up, and people who simply believe in you.

Additionally, part of your success will be based on the people you surround yourself with; when you associate with winning people it's a win-win for everyone. When they win you also win. You could be signed to a professional sports team and never play in one game, but if the team wins a championship you get the ring too. Live your life on winning teams!

IF THEY CAN YOU CAN

There are many incredible stories of people who found themselves in difficult situations but found the strength to recover.

Dave Pelzer's story comes to mind; he shared his story of child abuse in his book *A Child Called It: One Child's Courage to Survive*. I read this book as a teen but it has stayed with me because of Dave Pelzer's ability to recover from such a tortured childhood. In his mother's eyes he wasn't a child. She referred to him as "it". He has gone on to write many inspirational books and to inspire people to survive.

When describing his book Dave Pelzer says, "*A Child Called It* was a story about resilience, it was never about boo hoo hoo, it was about a kid that didn't quit."

GIVE THANKS

Speak thanks instead of complaints. Every moment is a perfect time to give thanks, but when you give thanks when you are feeling hopeless it shifts your focus from what is wrong to what is right in your life.

SEE IT AS A CHALLENGE

See setbacks as a challenge, an opportunity for you to grow and become stronger. There is much to be learned when you are down and when you feel out. It's true, what doesn't kill you will only make you STRONGER! And it is said that a smooth sea never made a skillful sailor.

Fierce people never take the "o'well" approach to life. Keep focused on your purpose in life, identify setbacks and recover. Reject thoughts and things that you know are not part of your destiny. Being defeated is not part of your purpose. You are a fighter! Build and never lose your resiliency.

Finish This Prayer: God, sometimes I want to give up, but…

List 5 people you admire that have shown resiliency in their lives:

1

___

___

2

___

___

3

___

___

4

___

___

5

___

___

A small guide to doing BIG things

List 5 things you are thankful for:

❶
_____
_____

❷
_____
_____

❸
_____
_____

❹
_____
_____

❺
_____
_____

Write 5 positive affirmations:

1

___

2

___

3

___

4

___

5

___

COMMITMENT

Commit.

"There's no abiding success without commitment."
Tony Robbins

Recently *ABC news* ran a story about how the marriage rate is declining, fewer people are committing to marriage. Fewer people are committing to anything. We live in a culture of the uncommitted. We all want to keep our options open, but ohhh... this is so detrimental to your success.

Without commitment you will fail. Claim your dreams, take ownership, and make an investment in them. Your dreams are too important to be on the fence and to half step with them.

When pilots are taking off on the runway they get to a point of commitment and they tell air traffic control "I am committed!" Meaning, if they do anything else at that point but attempt to fly they will crash.

ARE YOU A FLAKE?

In my book *30 things I Know for Certain* I talk about being a flake. A flake is someone who doesn't keep their word and someone who doesn't commit to anything. Do what you say you are going to do. You say you want to live your dreams? Just do it! Lack of commitment will only produce mediocre things.

If it's hard for you to stick to commitments make it personal. Promise yourself you will only give yourself the best. It is YOUR life. It is YOUR dreams. No one can be committed for you, only you can make the commitment.

COMMIT TO GOD

Get in covenant with God. Be committed to God and the plan he has for your life. Psalm 112 talks about the reward of the righteous.

> Praise ye the LORD. Blessed is the man that feareth the LORD, that delighteth greatly in his commandments.
>
> His seed shall be mighty upon earth: the generation of the upright shall be blessed.
>
> Wealth and riches shall be in his house: and his righteousness endureth for ever.
>
> Unto the upright there ariseth light in the darkness: he is gracious, and full of compassion, and righteous.
>
> A good man sheweth favour, and lendeth: he will guide his affairs with discretion.
>
> Surely he shall not be moved for ever: the righteous shall be in everlasting remembrance.
>
> He shall not be afraid of evil tidings: his heart is fixed, trusting in the LORD.

His heart is established, he shall not be afraid, until he see his desire upon his enemies.

He hath dispersed, he hath given to the poor; his righteousness endureth for ever; his horn shall be exalted with honour.

Fix your heart on God. There is nothing like living a blessed life! When you walk a committed life to God you will experience blessings you did not even sow, and insight into what to do in all areas of your life.

Sometimes I will get an idea or an understanding of something, and I know without a doubt that it is divine. Like, *no way I came up with that on my own!* You can try to figure things out on your own, but nothing compares to direction from God (especially when things are chaotic).

COMMIT TO HELPING OTHERS

The easiest thing to do in life is to look out for yourself. Yes, it's important to nourish your life. However, the easy route isn't always the best route. Go out of your way for someone else.

Success comes when there is significance in what you do, and significance is born when what you do helps someone else. Your dreams are about more than fame or fortune. Always use your platform for the purpose of dispersing something that is greater than yourself.

People often say what you make happen for others God will make happen for you. I believe this, but where people go wrong is that they replace "God" with "man". Give without expectation from man. God has your back. God will bless you!

When you give what you desire you put yourself in the position to receive it yourself.

There are three types of people on the ladder of success: those who climb it along, those who help others up with them, and those who kick others down. Help someone up as you climb the ladder of success. What is it that you do that can help someone else? And if you have to clobber and kick people down your final destination will not be success.

Albert Einstein said, "The value of a man resides in what he gives and NOT in what he is capable of receiving."

COMMIT TO WORK

At the beginning of this guide I asked you if you were the type of person who wishes or works for your dreams, because I can tell you a lot of fancy stuff but it means nothing if you are not willing to put in the work. Estee Lauder said, "I never dreamed about success. I worked for it."

Doing it big is hard work! It takes dedication and diligence. Day in and day out. When Ben Affleck won his Oscar® in 2013 he stood up in victory and said, "Work harder than you think you possibly can."

People say the secret to success is the Law of Attraction. I believe in visualizing (I even have a vision board, and encourage you to get one!), meditating, and thinking about the things that I want the universe to bring into my life. However, this fierce chick isn't just going to think about it, I am going to be about it. I am going to work for it!

Do you think Oprah just thinks about it? Do you

think Donald Trump just thinks about it? Do you think Mark Zuckerberg just thinks about it? Do you think Beyonce just thinks about it? No, they don't. You shouldn't either.

If the Law of Attraction is "the secret" the "real secret" is the Law of Work. This is what the Law of Work says: you get out what you put in. I know from personal experience that the Law of Work, well, works. Want evidence? You are holding evidence in your hand. I put in tons of work and BAM out came this book. Hustle, hustle, hustle!

Most people only see and want the sparkly side of success, but success comes by way of hard work. I use to watch *The Hills* on MTV and Kelly Cutrone, who owns the PR company People's Revolution, was a personality on the show. She dished out the best work advice, she urged the young socialites on the show to be workhorses and not show ponies.

Many people have amazing talent and great ideas but no focus or work ethic. It's tragic. Give yourself the opportunity to succeed. Be committed to being the hardest working person you know.

➥ Striking gold use to be as follows: 1. Travel west, 2. Dig. If only that was true today! Today it takes being extremely committed to the process because it might take a moment to strike gold. And then there are people who are not really serious about their dreams who are going to head home because the process is too long and too hard, and you are going to want to do the same thing. But hold up, you are committed to your dreams, heading home is no longer an option. You are in it for the long haul. This commitment is going to separate you from those who are sitting at home going through the motions of the ordinary, those who gave up and walked away. You, on the other hand, will keep digging! Dig!!! The reality of your dreams awaits you.

TRANSFORM THE PROMISE INTO REALITY

Someone at urbandictionary.com wrote the following when asked to define commitment:

> Commitment is what
> Transforms the promise into reality.
> It is the words that speak
> Boldly of your intentions.
> And the actions which speak
> Louder than the words.
> It is making the time
> When there is none.
> Coming through time
> After time after time,
> Year after year after year.
> Commitment is the stuff
> Character is made of;
> The power to change
> The face of things.
> It is the daily triumph
> Of integrity over skepticism.

Yes, it's the thing that must triumph every day. If you know what your purpose is in life you owe it to yourself to become committed to things that will propel you into the fullness of your purpose.

Make some things nonnegotiable. Stick to your dreams, you never know where they will lead you.

Finish This Prayer: God, I commit to you...

List 5 things you are completely committed to:

❶ _____
_____

❷ _____
_____

❸ _____
_____

❹ _____
_____

❺ _____
_____

List 5 ways you can help someone in the next week:

❶

_____

_____

❷

_____

_____

❸

_____

_____

❹

_____

_____

❺

_____

_____

What does being committed mean to you?

EVALUATION

Examine everything!

"A truthful evaluation of yourself gives feedback for growth and success."
Brenda Johnson Padgitt

I love Dr. Phil! I love how he keeps it real. One of his famous questions is, "So how is that working for you?" If you want to be fierce evaluate everything that makes up your life (and welcome constructive feedback from others!).

Put yourself on the couch and examine yourself. Self-examination will allow you to identify any barriers in your life that may be hindering you from reaching your full potential, holding you back from greatness.

It is scary to question everything, it will shake your core, but let the things that remain stay and the things that fall go.

The following is a list of questions to start the evaluation process. Not all questions will pertain to you, and of course this is not a complete list!

EVALUATE YOUR CHARACTER

What are your strengths?
What are your weaknesses?
Are you an honest person?
Do you have good morals?
Are you a nice person?
Are you lazy?

EVALUATE YOUR SPIRITUAL LIFE

What do you believe about God?
Are you thankful?
Are you growing spiritually?
Are you loving?

EVALUATE YOUR ATTITUDE

Do you expect good things to happen?
Do you complain a lot?
Do you look for the good in people?
Are you doubtful about everything?

EVALUATE YOUR RELATIONSHIPS

Do you enjoy your circle of friends?
Do you need to forgive someone?
Do you like how you treat your friends?
Are you giving to others?
Do you need to let someone go?
Do you allow people to use you?
Do you like your significant other?

EVALUATE YOUR BUSINESS

Do you need to rebrand?
Do you need to change your prices?
Do you need to do more networking?
Do you need to take a risk?

EVALUATE YOUR TALENT

How can you become better at what you do?
Are you defensive when someone offers up constructive feedback?
Do you invest time in improving your craft?

I DO MEAN EVERYTHING

Do you like your morning routine?
Do you like the clothes you wear?
Do you like where you live?
Do you like the car you drive?
Do you like the route you take to work?
Do you like the food you eat?

NO ONE IS PERFECT

This isn't about being perfect and having it all together, it is about being aware and making improvements.

One of my many problems is procrastination. I manage to meet deadlines but I put things off until the last minute, and create unnecessary stress. In my office I have a sign that says, "Procrastinate NOW!" to try to trick my mind into putting off procrastinating. Seriously, it's not a good thing! But I am aware of the situation. I know it is a weak area that I need to work on.

GIVE YOURSELF CREDIT

Evaluation should not just be about discovering what is wrong; it should also lead to identifying what is working well in your life. What do you need to do more of? How did you achieve your last achievement?

➡ You have achieved so much more than you give yourself credit for! Think about your successes, and know that you have it in you to create more!

BE A PROBLEM SOLVER

Evaluate and become a problem solver. Tinker with things. That is what mad scientist do, they are constantly problem solving and tinkering with projects they are working on. How can you make the project you are working on better? As a writer I do this all the time! I will write something, and go back and completely rewrite it (like this book!). I am saying the same thing, but only better. It's a process. Embrace the good-to-great process.

IGNORANCE IS BLISS

Ignorance is bliss, so I warn you that evaluation might reduce some of your bliss but it is how you improve, how you become better!

Finish This Prayer: God, allow me to see areas in my life where I can improve...

What are your weaknesses?

What are your strengths?

What makes you happy?

conclusion

Lose sight of the shore

"For I know the plans I have for you," declares
the Lord, "plans to prosper you and not to harm you,
plans to give you hope and a future."
Jeremiah 29:11 (NIV)

My biggest prayer for you is that you realize how much God loves you, and from that realization that you have the confidence to pursue your dreams and to fully live in your purpose. I challenge you to give your dreams to God and watch him turn them into something more, something beyond anything you could ever imagine!

Start now on your dreams, live life without regrets! You are FIERCE and you can DO BIG THINGS!

L♥VE,
Gloria Marie Pelcher
gm@gloriamarie.com

JOURNAL

It's up to you! Write whatever your soul needs to let out! Write whatever God puts on your heart. Habakkuk 2:2 says, "And the LORD answered me, and said, Write the vision, and make it plain upon tables, that he may run that readeth it." Write down your reflections, your ideas, your ahas, your business plans, your affirmations, your declarations, your intuitions, just go for it!

_____

_____

_____

_____

_____

_____

_____

_____

A small guide to doing BIG things

FIERCE

A small guide to doing BIG things

FIERCE

A small guide to doing BIG things

FIERCE

A small guide to doing BIG things

A small guide to doing BIG things

FIERCE

A small guide to doing BIG things

FIERCE

A small guide to doing BIG things

FIERCE

A small guide to doing BIG things

A small guide to doing BIG things

A small guide to doing BIG things

A small guide to doing BIG things

A small guide to doing BIG things

FIERCE

A small guide to doing BIG things

A small guide to doing BIG things

FIERCE

A small guide to doing BIG things

FIERCE

A small guide to doing BIG things

FIERCE

A small guide to doing BIG things

A small guide to doing BIG things

A small guide to doing BIG things

FAITH

A small guide to doing BIG things

INTENT

A small guide to doing BIG things

EDUCATION

A small guide to doing BIG things

RESILIENCE

FIERCE

A small guide to doing BIG things

COMMITMENT

EVALUATION

FIERCE

Cut out and post somewhere to remind yourself just how fierce you are!

I AM FIERCE

About Gloria Marie Pelcher

GLORIA MARIE PELCHER lives in Dallas, TX. She is a teacher, speaker, photographer, writer, business owner, and has published multiple books, including *GIVE everything*, and she blogs regularly at gloriamarie.com. Her mission is to inspire you to DREAM & live your purpose!™

Join The #dreamteam!
gloriamarie.com/dreamteam

Connect!

gloriamarie.com
twitter.com/gloriamarie
facebook.com/gloriamarie
goodreads.com/gloriamarie
instagram.com/gloriamarie

If you are interested in having Gloria Marie Pelcher speak at your next event visit gloriamarie.com/events

www.ingramcontent.com/pod-product-compliance
Lightning Source LLC
Chambersburg PA
CBHW060327050426
42449CB00011B/2689